EAT SMART

MILK AND DAIRY

Louise Spilsbury

Heinemann Library
Chicago, Illinois

Library of Congress Cataloging-in-Publication Data
Spilsbury, Louise.
  Milk and dairy / Louise Spilsbury.
     p. cm. -- (Eat smart)
  Includes bibliographical references and index.
  ISBN 978-1-4329-1813-2 (hc) -- ISBN 978-1-4329-1820-0 (pb) 1. Dairy products--Juvenile literature. 2. Cookery (Dairy products)--Juvenile literature. I. Title.
  TX377.S75 2009
  641.3'7--dc22
                          2008045003

Acknowledgments
We would like to thank the following for permission to reproduce photographs: © Alamy pp. **4** (Corbis), **16** (Jupiterimages/Brand X), **18** (UpperCut Images); © Corbis p. **11** (Herve Hughes/Hemis); © Getty Images pp. **7** (Stone/Tim Flach), **12** (Photographer's Choice/Barry Yee); © iStock pp. **1–32** background images; © Masterfile p. **14** (Royalty Free); © Pearson Education Ltd/MM Studios pp. **9, 17, 20, 21, 22, 24, 25** top, **25** bottom, **26, 27** top, **27** bottom, **28, 29** top, **29** bottom; © Photolibrary pp. **6** (The Irish Image Collection), **19** (Stockbyte); © Punchstock p. **15** (Photodisc); © Science Photolibrary pp. **5** (Mauro Fermariello), **8** (James Kirs-Holmes), **10** (Rosenfeld Images Ltd), **13** (Roger Harris).

Cover photograph reproduced with permission of © Getty Images (Lew Robertson).

Every effort has been made to contact copyright holders of material reproduced in this book. Any omissions will be rectified in subsequent printings if notice is given to the publishers.

CONTENTS

Some words are shown in bold, **like this**. You can find out what they mean by looking in the glossary.

WHAT ARE DAIRY FOODS?

Dairy foods include milk and certain products made from milk, such as cheese and yogurt. Most milk and dairy foods consumed by people in North America, Europe, and Australia come from cows.

When did people start drinking milk?

People first began to keep animals for their meat around 8,000 years ago. Later, they started to consume the milk produced by some of these farm animals as well. **Neolithic** farmers in Britain and northern Europe may have been some of the first people to begin using cattle milk, around 6,000 years ago. There is also evidence that ancient Sumerians, who lived in the region that is now the Middle East, made milk into cheese 5,000 years ago.

▲ There is a wide range of milk and dairy products to choose from today, including different flavored cheeses, fruit and sweetened yogurts, and a choice of milk.

Why is it smart to eat dairy foods?

It is smart to drink milk and eat some dairy foods because they contain **nutrients**. Nutrients are substances that the human body needs to develop properly and to stay healthy. The nutrients in dairy foods help your body to grow and maintain strong bones. They also help your muscles and nerves to work properly.

Milk around the world

Animals that produce milk to feed their young are called **mammals**. Around the world, people drink or use milk from many female mammals other than cows. In some places, people keep goats or sheep for milk. People make cheese from yak milk in Tibet, goat milk in Switzerland, buffalo milk in Egypt, and reindeer milk in Arctic regions!

Milk products such as cheese can come from a number of different mammals. This woman is milking a goat.

WHERE DO DAIRY FOODS COME FROM?

All female **mammals**, including humans, produce milk to feed their young in the early months of a baby's life. Farms where female cows are reared for their milk are called dairy farms. The fresh milk you buy usually takes less than two days to get from the dairy farm to the store.

How do dairy farms work?

The first milk a cow produces for its calf is rich in extra **nutrients**. These help a calf grow fast and gain strength quickly and also protect it from disease. A few days after a calf has been born, dairy farmers start to feed it a milk substitute. They do this for six to eight weeks, until the calf can start to eat solid foods such as grains. This means the farmer can take milk from a cow to sell soon after her calves have been born.

 Healthy cows can produce over 5 gallons (20 liters) of milk every day for around 10 months after giving birth.

Hungry cows!

In order to be able to produce milk, a cow needs to take in a lot of nutrients herself. Cows may spend 8 to 10 hours a day eating grass or grains such as barley and oats. To help them **digest** all this food, they can drink enough water to fill a bathtub every day!

A herd of cows is usually milked twice a day—in the morning and in the evening. Milking never hurts the cow.

How is milk collected?

On a modern dairy farm, electric-powered milking machines have tubes attached to sets of rubber cups. These cups are attached to the cow's teats— the parts calves suck on to get milk. The milking machine mimics the natural sucking action of a calf, and this pumps milk from the cows into the tubes. The milk passes through the tubes into large tanks, where it is cooled and stored. The milk is then collected by giant refrigerated tankers that transport the milk to a dairy factory.

How is milk treated?

After milk arrives at a dairy factory, it is **pasteurized**. Pasteurization is a process in which milk is heated rapidly to kill off any harmful **bacteria** that might be in the raw milk. Bacteria are microscopic living things that could make people sick, so it is especially important that young and old people, or women who are pregnant, do not drink unpasteurized milk.

Milk consists of tiny droplets of cream, which is a type of fat, and water. Fresh milk that is bottled right after pasteurization is known as whole milk. Semi-skimmed (2%) milk has about half the milk fat removed, and skimmed milk is milk from which almost all the fat has been removed. Semi-skimmed and skimmed milk are smart choices for a healthy diet because they are less fatty, but still have all of the nutrients of whole milk.

Today, most fresh milk is sold in plastic bottles like these. The plastic is clear, so you can see the amount of milk left inside. The bottles are easily resealable and shaped to fit into most refrigerator doors. Most also have a handle for carrying and pouring.

What other kinds of milk are there?

When kept in a refrigerator, fresh milk lasts about 14 days, at most, from the time it is bought. Some milk is **processed** to make it last longer.

Powdered milk is milk from which all the liquid is removed so that it is completely dried out. To turn powdered milk into milk again, you simply add water. Powdered milk should be refrigerated after being mixed with water.

Vacuum-packed milk undergoes a special process that takes most of the oxygen out of the package. This type of milk can last for several months to a year without being refrigerated.

 Milk needs to be kept cold to stay fresh, but if this is not possible then powdered milk mixed with water is a useful alternative. Whole powdered milk contains all the nutrients of whole milk in a concentrated form.

Camel's milk, anyone?

There could soon be camel's milk on supermarket shelves in countries in North America and Europe. The **United Nations** has called for camel's milk, which is drunk widely in the Middle East, to be sold in other places because it is particularly high in nutrients.

How is yogurt made?

Yogurt is made by the action of certain live bacteria on milk. When these bacteria are added to milk and the milk is warmed and left for a while, the bacteria cause the **lactose** (a type of sugar) in the milk to produce lactic **acid**. The lactic acid reacts with **proteins** in the milk to form semi-solid yogurt. Some yogurts are then pasteurized to kill the bacteria before they are sold, but others contain the live bacteria.

Bacteria are added to milk in these big tanks to produce yogurt.

How is cheese made?

Before there were refrigerators, cheese was a way of storing milk. People make cheese by mixing and heating milk with acids and **rennet**. These substances make the milk slightly sour and cause it to separate into solid lumps, called curds, and watery liquid, called whey. Salt is added to the curds and they are pressed into molds (containers) to form cheese. The cheese is then left to mature.

Discovering cheese

No one knows exactly how or when people discovered cheese. One legend says that thousands of years ago a man filled a saddlebag with milk to sustain him on a desert journey. When he stopped to drink, the milk had separated into curds and whey. The milk had reacted with rennet from the saddlebag, which was made from an animal's stomach!

Some cheeses are ready to eat in days, while other cheeses take months or even years to get to the desired flavor and texture.

Types of cheese

Different kinds of cheese are formed in different ways. Hard cheeses such as cheddar have a natural dry rind (skin), which forms as the curds on the surface dry out. People make soft cheeses such as Brie by washing the surface with harmless **molds**. These grow on the outside of the cheese to make a soft, white rind. Blue cheese has harmless molds injected into it. The length of time cheese is left to ripen also affects its taste and texture.

WHY ARE DAIRY FOODS GOOD FOR YOU?

One of the main reasons why dairy foods such as milk, yogurt, and cheese are good for you is because they are a good source of **calcium**. Calcium is a very important **nutrient** that the body needs. Cream and butter contain much less calcium.

 The human body cannot make its own calcium, so you must drink and eat foods that contain calcium every day.

Calcium counts!

To get the same amount of calcium as you do from a 7-fluid-ounce (200-milliliter) glass of milk, you would need to eat four servings of broccoli, eleven servings of spinach, or seven slices of bread! Often, the calcium in these vegetables and grains is not absorbed as easily as the calcium in milk and milk products.

What is calcium?

Calcium is a **mineral**. Plants take in minerals when they soak water up from the ground through their roots. Humans and other animals take in minerals when they eat plants or meat from animals that have eaten plants. Minerals from the plants that cows and other **mammals** eat are also present in their milk.

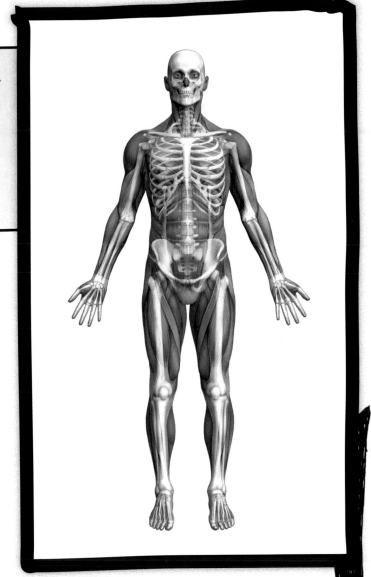

Calcium-rich bones are strong and compact. Low calcium intake results in weak bones because the body takes calcium stored in bones to use elsewhere—for example, in muscles and nerves.

Why do you need calcium?

You need calcium so your body can build strong bones and teeth.

The bones in the skeleton form a framework that holds the body together. Along with your muscles, bones also allow you to move.

Strong, healthy teeth are very important because they enable you to eat a variety of different foods. Foods begin to break up in the mouth during chewing, which makes it easier to swallow and **digest** food.

What else does calcium do?

Calcium is necessary for blood to **clot** during bleeding and it helps the heart beat properly to keep blood moving around the body. You also need calcium to make your muscles contract. Calcium also helps with the functioning of the **nervous system**, which carries messages to and from the brain to the rest of your body.

Why does calcium help bones grow?

Calcium is hard and makes bones strong and rigid, to support the body's weight. Extra calcium builds up in bones as you grow up. Calcium makes children's bones grow as they get taller. People stop growing in height at the age of about 20. You continue to build bone until you are around 25 to 30 years old. After that, the body uses its calcium to make bones stronger and more compact, and to repair broken bones or replace worn-out bone **cells**. Building healthy bones by getting plenty of calcium and exercise when you are young reduces the risk of brittle bone disease, or **osteoporosis**, in later life.

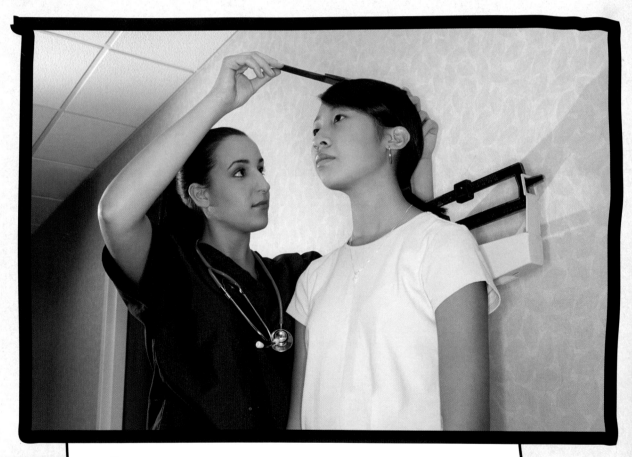

Milk and dairy foods contain **proteins** essential for growth and the mineral zinc, which helps with growth during childhood.

Brushing your teeth twice a day will remove the bacteria that can rob teeth of the calcium that makes them hard and strong.

How does calcium make teeth strong?

Calcium is one of the substances that make up the hard parts of your teeth. The toughest part of your teeth is the surface **enamel**. This is 97 percent calcium. If you do not brush your teeth properly, **bacteria** build up on the teeth and change the sugars in food into **acid**. Acid is a strong substance that can slowly dissolve the calcium in your teeth enamel. This is how cavities (holes) in the teeth form.

Calcium on the move

There is more calcium in your body than any other mineral. About 99 percent of the body's calcium is found in the bones and teeth. Bones store calcium and release some of it into the blood when it is needed. The blood carries it to other parts of the body that have to use it, such as the muscles and nerves.

Other nutrients in dairy foods

Milk and milk products also contain protein. Protein is a nutrient that gives the body the materials it needs for growth and repair. Dairy foods also contain useful **vitamins**. For example, vitamin A helps to protect the body against diseases and keeps the eyes and skin healthy. Some dairy foods contain vitamin D, which helps the body to absorb calcium from food. Vitamin B12 helps maintain healthy nerves and blood cells.

It is always important to eat foods containing calcium, but this is especially important when you have broken bones, because the body uses calcium to rebuild the bone.

Milk foods and fat

Some foods made from milk, such as butter, cream, cream cheese, full-fat ice cream, and whipped cream, contain mostly fat and are not considered good sources of calcium. You need some fat to be healthy, but if you eat too much fat you can become overweight. This is bad for the heart and can make you unhealthy, so you should limit the amount of these milk products you eat.

To reduce the amount of fat in your diet, put only a thin scraping of butter on your bread or toast.

Dairy alternatives

Some people choose not to drink milk or eat dairy foods, or they cannot because they are **allergic** to them. These people can get calcium from other sources, including **soy milk** products enriched with calcium, dark green leafy vegetables, almonds or sesame seeds, dried fruits such as apricots, and fish that have soft edible bones in them, such as sardines.

No milk, thank you

In some parts of the world, milk is not traditionally part of an adult's diet. Many people have **lactose** intolerance and are unable to **digest** or absorb lactose sugar in milk. In South America, Africa, and Asia, more than half of the population is intolerant to lactose, and in some parts of Asia almost no one drinks milk!

WHAT IS THE BEST WAY TO EAT DAIRY FOODS?

You can drink milk and eat dairy foods in a variety of ways. Try a range of dairy foods in different recipes to make your meals more interesting, but remember that most dairy foods are fresh and need to be stored carefully.

Storing dairy foods

You should store most milk and other dairy products in a refrigerator to keep them fresh and safe to eat. That is why you should check the "use by" dates on dairy products, particularly milk and cream. Never drink or eat dairy foods that are out of date, because they may make you sick.

Fresh milk keeps for between three and five days once it has been opened, but you should store it in containers that can be resealed. Hard cheeses keep for longer than soft cheeses, but even so, you should buy small amounts of cheese at a time and eat them when they are fresh.

Milk tastes best served cold, straight from the refrigerator. Storing milk in a refrigerator keeps it fresh, too, so put it back right away after you have poured yourself some.

Healthy choices

If you are watching your weight, low-fat milk or dairy products are a healthy choice because they contain less fat but still have the same amount of **calcium** and other **nutrients** as full-fat versions. Avoid malted or flavored milk drinks or desserts that contain too much added sugar.

You should also choose dairy products that contain little or no salt. This is because too much salt can cause high **blood pressure**, which can result in heart disease when you are older.

Flavored milk is nutritious and makes a tasty treat, but choose one that does not have too much added sugar and that is lower in fat.

Cheese-loving countries

French and Greek people are the world's largest consumers of cheese. In France and Greece, people eat around 50 pounds (28 kilograms) of cheese a year. In Greece, around three-quarters of the cheese eaten is feta, a salty cheese made from sheep's and goat's milk. In France, one of the most popular varieties is the soft cow's cheese known as camembert.

Using milk

You can drink fresh milk alone or mix it with fresh fruit to make a smoothie. To drink more milk, have a glass with your meals, ideally semi-skimmed (2%) or skimmed milk. Cooking with milk gives food a creamy taste and texture. Milk can be used to make white sauces, puddings, and pancakes, or it can be stirred into soups. You could also add milk instead of water to oatmeal and other hot cereals.

Eat more yogurt

A tub or bowl of yogurt makes a quick and healthy dessert or snack between meals, especially if you choose a yogurt with no added sugar and top it with some chopped-up fruit such as strawberries. You can serve plain yogurt with a little honey, mixed with granola, or in place of cream with a dessert. You can also add yogurt to soups and stews and use it in vegetable sauces and dips. A baked potato topped with fat-free or low-fat yogurt could be part of a light and healthy dinner.

A bowl of fruit, yogurt, and granola makes a healthy breakfast or snack.

A baked potato topped with grated cheese and served with a salad is a nutritious and easy meal to make. It will supply you with a balance of nutrients, including a portion of calcium.

Cooking with cheese

Cheese can be used in sandwiches, and it is also a useful ingredient in cooking. Most cheese, particularly hard cheese, is strongly flavored, so a little can go a long way. Many people grate cheese and sprinkle it onto pasta, stir a little into a sauce, or sprinkle it on top of casseroles, soups, stews, or vegetables. Cheese can also be the main feature of a dish, as in cheese omelettes and soufflés, or when chopped into cubes and added to salad.

Cheese rolling

One of the more unusual uses for cheese is cheese-rolling competitions! In these competitions, people from cheese-making communities chase large, round blocks of cheese down a steep hill to see which gets to the bottom first!

HOW MUCH DAIRY FOOD SHOULD YOU EAT?

Milk and dairy foods are a very important part of most people's daily diet. To eat smart, you should be aware of which types of foods and drinks are included in the milk and dairy food group. Milk, yogurt, and **calcium**-enriched **soy milk** and soy milk products all count, but low-calcium, high-fat milk products such as butter, cream, and ice cream do not.

What counts as a portion?

The easiest way to achieve your daily calcium requirement is to eat or drink three portions of milk and dairy foods a day. The size of a portion of dairy food depends on how concentrated that food is. For example, one serving of milk is almost 7 fluid ounces (200 milliliters), one serving of yogurt is over 5 ounces (150 milliliters), and one serving of cheese is 1 ounce (30 grams), which is about a matchbox-sized piece of cheese. Choose lower fat alternatives such as skimmed and semi-skimmed (2%) milk whenever possible, or eat higher fat versions less often or in smaller amounts.

What is a balanced diet?

Milk and dairy foods provide only some of the **nutrients** people need. A balanced diet contains a variety of foods that together provide all the nutrients people need to be healthy. The food plate diagram (opposite) shows the types and proportions of foods needed for a well-balanced diet. It shows how people should eat lots of fruits and vegetables, plenty of grains and other **starchy carbohydrate** foods such as bread, rice, pasta, and potatoes, some milk and dairy foods, some **proteins** such as meat, fish, eggs, and beans, and just a small amount of foods and drinks that are high in fat or sugar.

Top tip

One way to ensure you eat calcium-rich dairy foods each day is to eat some with every meal. Try milk with cereal for breakfast, a cheese and lettuce sandwich for lunch, and a yogurt for dessert after dinner in the evening.

If you want to eat smart and be healthy, try to think about the proportions of the different foods you eat in a day. Look at the "MyPyramid" food pyramid diagram above.

Milk and Dairy Recipes

Fruit smoothie

This fruit smoothie is packed with dairy and fruit. Use chilled milk and yogurt for a cool, fresh taste.

Ingredients

- 10 fl oz. (275 mL) cold semi-skimmed (2 %) milk
- 5 fl oz. (150 mL) low-fat yogurt
- 1 banana
- 4 large strawberries
- 1 tablespoon honey

Equipment

- Measuring cup
- Blender
- Small knife
- Chopping board
- A tall drinking glass

WHAT YOU DO

1 Pour the milk and the yogurt into the blender.

2 Peel the banana and add to the blender.

Always ask an adult to help you in the kitchen.

EAT SMART

3 Wash the strawberries and cut the green stalks off. Place the strawberries in the blender with the honey.

4 Put the lid on the blender and switch on for periods of 5–10 seconds. Repeat this until the mixture is smooth.

5 Pour the smoothie into the glass.

New smoothies
You can use different fruits with the yogurt and milk to create new smoothies. Try raspberries or a mixture of blueberries and blackberries instead of the strawberries, for example.

Potato and leek gratin

This recipe for potatoes baked in milk and sour cream is rich in **calcium**. It makes a balanced meal if served with a green salad or vegetables such as broccoli and carrots. It should serve six people.

Ingredients

- 10 fl oz. (275 mL) milk
- 4 cloves garlic
- 1 bay leaf
- 1/8 teaspoon nutmeg
- 1½ teaspoons salt
- Freshly ground black pepper to taste
- 6 medium-sized potatoes
- 1 teaspoon olive oil
- 3 medium-sized leeks
- 2 tablespoons sour cream
- 1 tablespoon Dijon mustard
- 2 oz. (50 g) strong cheddar cheese

Equipment

- Pastry brush
- A shallow 2-quart (2-liter) baking dish
- Knife
- Measuring cup
- A large, heavy-bottomed saucepan
- Frying pan
- Slotted spoon
- Cheese grater
- Oven mitts

WHAT YOU DO

1 **Preheat** the oven to 425°F (220°C). Brush a little oil over the inside of the baking dish.

2 Peel the potatoes and cut them into slices ¼ inch (0.5 cm) thick.

3 Peel and cut the garlic into small pieces. Put the milk, garlic, bay leaf, nutmeg, salt, and pepper into the saucepan. Bring this to a simmer (so it is bubbling gently) over medium-low heat, stirring all the time.

Always ask an adult to help you in the kitchen.

4 Gently add the potatoes to the pan and simmer gently over a low heat, stirring often, until the potatoes are just cooked but not soft. This should take about 5–10 minutes.

5 Peel off the top layer from the leeks and cut off the roots from the bottom and the shoots from the top. Wash the leeks carefully and then cut them into thin slices. Heat the oil in a frying pan over medium-low heat. Add the leeks and fry them for 5 minutes or until tender.

6 Use a slotted spoon to transfer half the cooked potatoes to the oiled baking dish. Cover with the leek mixture. Then spread the rest of the potatoes over the leeks.

7 Remove the bay leaf from the milk in the pan. Stir the sour cream and mustard into the milk. Spread this over the vegetables in the baking dish.

8 Grate the cheese and sprinkle it over the top of the milk mixture.

9 Bake for 20–25 minutes, until the cheese is bubbly and golden on top.

Rice pudding

This creamy rice pudding is rich in calcium from the milk. The rice makes it filling and the fruit gives some added **nutrients** as well as sweetness.

Ingredients

- 19 fl oz. (570 mL) whole milk
- 2 cups (275 g) dried apricots or prunes
- 3/4 cup (110 g) plain white rice

Equipment

- Large oven dish
- Knife
- Chopping board
- Measuring cup
- Mixing bowl
- Oven mitts

WHAT YOU DO

1 Preheat the oven to 350°F (180°C).

2 Chop the dried fruit into small pieces.

3 Put the fruit, rice, and milk into a bowl and mix together.

4 Pour into the oven-proof dish and cook for 40 minutes.

5 Leave to cool a little before serving warm.

Tip!
Grate nutmeg over the top of the pudding before you cook it. In addition to adding flavor, the nutmeg browns the top of the pudding when it cooks.

GLOSSARY

acid substance with a sour, bitter taste

allergic get a physical reaction to a (usually harmless) substance. Allergic reactions can range from mild, such as sneezing or a rash, to severe, such as breathing difficulties.

bacteria extremely small organisms that can only be seen using a microscope. Some bacteria can cause disease or sickness.

blood pressure force exerted by the heart in pumping blood around the body

calcium mineral used by the body to help maintain bones and teeth. Calcium also has an important role in muscle contraction, blood clotting, and nerve function.

carbohydrate type of nutrient found in food. The body breaks carbohydrates down into sugars that it uses for energy.

cell all living things are made up of millions of microscopic parts called cells. Different parts of the body are made up of different types of cells.

clot form a clump in a liquid

digest name for the way the stomach, intestine, and other body parts work together to break down food into pieces so small they dissolve in liquid and pass into the blood

enamel hard white substance that covers the part of a tooth above the gum

lactose type of sugar found in milk and milk products

mammal warm-blooded animal with hair on its skin. Female mammals give birth to live young and feed their babies on milk from their own body.

mineral substance that comes from non-living sources, such as rocks that break down and become part of the soil. Some of the nutrients that plants take in through their roots are called minerals.

mold type of fungus (plant-like organism) that can only be seen under a microscope. Molds can help cheese mature and enhance its flavor.

Neolithic from the period around 8,000 to 5,000 BCE, when people started farming and keeping livestock for food and lived in settled communities

nervous system system of nerves that regulates and coordinates all the body's activities

nutrient substance found in food that is essential for life

osteoporosis condition caused by a loss of calcium and other substances from bones, making them weak and prone to breaks or fractures

pasteurize heat liquids in order to destroy harmful substances such as bacteria. The process was named after its inventor, the French scientist Louis Pasteur (1822–1895).

preheat heat an oven to the recommended temperature before cooking in it

processed prepared and changed from a natural state to make a new product, such as when milk is processed into cheese or meat is processed into sausages

protein nutrient that provides the raw materials the body needs to grow and repair itself

rennet substance taken from the stomachs of calves and lambs. It is used to make milk separate into solids (curds) and liquid (whey) when making cheese. Vegetarian cheeses are made using rennet from either fungal or bacterial sources.

soy milk milk made from soybeans, which are a good source of protein

starchy something containing starch. Starch is a plant's store of excess glucose (food).

United Nations international organization comprising most of the nations of the world. It was formed in 1945 with the aim to promote peace, security, health, and economic development in all countries.

vacuum space with little or no air in it. "Vacuum packed" means packaging that has had all of the air removed from it before being sealed.

vitamin nutrient people require to grow and stay healthy

FIND OUT MORE

At **www.cnpp.usda.gov**, a site from the Center for Nutrition Policy and Promotion, there is information about health and nutrition. Included is the "MyPyramid" food pyramid, which offers guidelines for a healthy, balanced diet. Explore the pyramid to find the right serving sizes for your age.

At **www.nutrition.gov**, an educational site set up by the U.S. Department of Agriculture, learn more about nutrition.

At **kidshealth.org/kid** there is a large section on staying healthy and some recipes to try.

INDEX

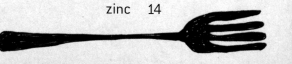